Don't Get Duped

A Consumer's Guide to Avoiding Scams

James H. Foster

©2023

Table of content

Chapter 1: Introduction to Scams

Welcome to the world of scams, where deception lurks around every corner and unsuspecting consumers are the targets. In this chapter, we will explore the importance of consumer awareness, the common types of scams you may encounter, the psychological manipulation employed by scammers, and the consequences of falling for their tricks. So buckle up and get ready to arm yourself with knowledge to avoid getting duped!

Importance of Consumer Awareness

Scams have become more prevalent than ever, thanks to the digital age we live in. It is crucial for consumers to be aware of the various scams out there, as this knowledge serves as an armor against fraudsters. By understanding the tactics scammers use, you can better protect yourself and your hard-earned money. Remember, knowledge is power!

Let me share a personal experience to emphasize the importance of consumer awareness. A close friend of mine, let's call her Sarah, received an email claiming to be from her bank. The email stated that her account had been compromised and urged her to click on a link to resolve the issue. Sarah was alarmed and clicked on the link without giving it a second thought. Little did she know, she had just fallen into the trap of a phishing scam.

Tip to prevent falling for phishing scams: Always be cautious of unsolicited emails, especially those asking for personal information or directing you to click on suspicious links. Instead of clicking on the link provided, go directly to the official website of the organization in question and verify the information there.

Overview of Common Types of Scams

Scammers are constantly coming up with new ways to deceive unsuspecting victims. From online dating scams to phone scams and everything in between, it's essential to be aware of the common types of scams.

Let's take a look at one of the most common types of scams: the tech support scam. Imagine you receive a phone call from someone claiming to be from a well-known tech company. They inform you that your computer has been infected with a virus and offer to help you fix the issue for a fee. In reality, they are just trying to gain access to your personal and financial information.

Tip to avoid falling for tech support scams: Remember, legitimate tech companies will never proactively call you to fix issues with your computer. If you ever receive such a call, hang up immediately and contact the official support channels of the company to verify the legitimacy of the call.

Psychological Manipulation in Scams

Scammers are master manipulators, using psychological tactics to exploit their victims' vulnerabilities. They prey on our emotions, such as fear, greed, and urgency, to push us into making impulsive decisions.

Let's dive into an example to understand how scammers manipulate our emotions. Imagine you receive a call from someone claiming to be a law enforcement officer, stating that there is an arrest warrant out for you due to unpaid taxes. They create a sense of fear and urgency, pressuring you to make an immediate payment to avoid legal consequences. In reality, it's just a scammer trying to steal your money.

Tip to protect yourself from fear-based scams: Always take a step back and assess the situation calmly. If someone claims to be from a legitimate organization, ask for their contact information and verify it independently before taking any action.

Consequences of Falling for Scams

Falling for a scam can have devastating consequences, both financially and emotionally. Scammers often target vulnerable individuals, such as the elderly or those experiencing financial difficulties. The aftermath of a scam can leave victims feeling violated, embarrassed, and even traumatized.

To illustrate the consequences of falling for scams, let me share the story of John, a retiree who lost his life savings to an investment scam. John was approached by a smooth-talking fraudster who promised incredible returns on his investment. Blinded by the prospect of financial security, John handed over his hard-earned money, only to realize later that it was all a sham.

Tip to avoid falling for investment scams: Remember the saying, "If it sounds too good to be true, it probably is." Conduct thorough research, seek advice from trusted financial advisors, and never invest in something you don't fully understand.

Now that you understand the importance of consumer awareness, the common types of scams, the psychological manipulation employed by scammers, and the consequences of falling for their tricks, you're ready to dive deeper into the specific scams and learn how to protect yourself. So let's move on to Chapter 2: Online Dating Scams, where we'll explore the treacherous waters of online romance and how to navigate them safely.

Chapter 2: Online Dating Scams

Popular Tactics Used by Scammers

Online dating has become increasingly popular in recent years, opening up new avenues for scammers to prey on unsuspecting individuals. These scammers are skilled at manipulating emotions and creating fake personas to lure their victims into a web of deception. Here are some popular tactics used by scammers in online dating:

Recognizing Fake Profiles

Spotting fake profiles can be challenging, but there are a few telltale signs that can help you identify scammers:

Warning Signs in Online Conversations

When engaging in online conversations, be vigilant for the following warning signs that may indicate a potential scam:

Protective Measures for Online Daters

To protect yourself from online dating scams, it's essential to take proactive measures. Here are some practical steps to safeguard your personal information and avoid falling victim to scams:

Remember, online dating can be a wonderful way to connect with others, but it's important to approach it with caution. By staying vigilant and following these protective measures, you can reduce the risk of falling victim to online dating scams.

Chapter 3: Online Shopping Scams

In this chapter, we will delve into the world of online shopping scams and equip you with the knowledge and tools to protect yourself from falling victim to these fraudulent schemes. We will explore how to identify fake online stores, recognize red flags in product listings, ensure payment security, and take appropriate actions if scammed. By the end of this chapter, you will be able to shop online with confidence and avoid becoming a target for scammers.

Identifying Fake Online Stores

Have you ever stumbled upon an online store that seemed too good to be true? Chances are, it probably was. Fake online stores are a prevalent breeding ground for scams, where fraudsters create enticing websites to lure unsuspecting shoppers. These scam artists use various tactics to deceive consumers and steal their hard-earned money.

Anecdote: Picture this - you're searching for a new smartphone online and stumble upon a website offering the latest model at an unbelievably low price. Excited by the deal, you hastily make the purchase, only to receive a counterfeit phone or nothing at all. This unfortunate scenario is all too common among online shoppers who fall prey to fake online stores.

To avoid falling into this trap, here are a few key indicators to look out for:

Red Flags in Product Listings

When browsing through online shopping platforms, it's crucial to scrutinize product listings carefully. Scammers often use deceptive tactics to lure unsuspecting buyers into purchasing counterfeit or non-existent products. By familiarizing yourself with the red flags, you can avoid falling victim to these scams.

Anecdote: Imagine eagerly ordering a designer handbag from an online marketplace, only to receive a cheap knockoff that falls apart within days. This frustrating experience highlights the importance of being vigilant when evaluating product listings.

Here are a few red flags to watch out for:

Payment Security in Online Shopping

When it comes to online shopping, ensuring payment security is paramount. Scammers are constantly devising new ways to steal sensitive financial information, which can lead to identity theft or unauthorized transactions. By adopting a few protective measures, you can safeguard your payment details and minimize the risk of falling victim to online shopping scams.

Anecdote: Close your eyes for a moment and imagine receiving your credit card statement, only to find a series of unauthorized charges from unknown online stores. This nightmarish scenario serves as a stark reminder of the importance of securing your payment information.

Here are some practical steps to enhance payment security:

Steps to Take if Scammed

Despite our best efforts, there is always a chance of falling victim to an online shopping scam. If you find yourself in such a situation, it's essential to take immediate action to minimize the damage and increase the chances of recovering your funds.

Anecdote: Imagine ordering a highly anticipated gadget online, only to receive an empty package. The sinking feeling of being scammed can be overwhelming, but remember, there are steps you can take to rectify the situation.

If you have been scammed, here's what you can do:

Remember, prevention is the best defense against online shopping scams. By staying informed, being cautious, and following the protective measures outlined in this chapter, you can shop online with confidence and minimize the risk of falling victim to fraudsters. Stay vigilant, trust your instincts, and remember, if a deal seems too good to be true, it probably is.

Chapter 4: Investment Scams

Investing can be a great way to grow your wealth and secure your financial future. However, it's important to be aware of the potential risks and pitfalls that come with investing, especially when it comes to investment scams. In this chapter, we will explore common investment fraud schemes, provide tips for recognizing promising versus risky investments, discuss how to research and verify investment opportunities, and offer guidance on reporting investment scams.

Common Investment Fraud Schemes

Investment scams come in many different forms, and scammers are constantly coming up with new tactics to deceive unsuspecting investors. Some common investment fraud schemes include:

Recognizing Promising versus Risky Investments

One of the key skills in avoiding investment scams is being able to distinguish between promising investment opportunities and risky ventures. Here are some tips to help you make informed investment decisions:

Researching and Verifying Investment Opportunities

To protect yourself from investment scams, it's crucial to research and verify any investment opportunities before committing your money. Here are some steps you can take:

Reporting Investment Scams

If you believe you have fallen victim to an investment scam or have encountered a suspicious investment opportunity, it's important to report it. By reporting scams, you not only protect yourself but also help authorities identify and take action against scammers. Here are some steps to take:

Remember, the best defense against investment scams is knowledge and skepticism. Stay informed, ask questions, and always trust your instincts. By taking the time to research and verify investment opportunities, you can protect yourself and your hard-earned money from scammers.

Chapter 5: Phone Scams

The ringing of a phone can be a source of excitement or annoyance, depending on who's calling. But what if the person on the other end of the line is trying to scam you? Phone scams have become increasingly prevalent in recent years, with scammers using clever tactics to deceive unsuspecting victims. In this chapter, we will explore the popular types of phone scams, teach you how to identify caller ID spoofing, provide tips on responding to unsolicited calls, and offer effective ways to prevent falling victim to phone scams.

Popular Types of Phone Scams

Phone scams come in various forms, each with its own unique approach to deceive and defraud. Some of the most common types of phone scams include:

Identifying Caller ID Spoofing

Caller ID spoofing is a technique used by scammers to manipulate the caller ID display on your phone. They can make it appear as if they are calling from a different number, often a legitimate organization or government agency, to gain your trust and increase the likelihood of you falling for their scam.

To identify caller ID spoofing, pay attention to the following signs:

Responding to Unsolicited Calls

When you receive an unsolicited call, it's crucial to remain calm and take the following steps to protect yourself:

Preventing Phone Scams

While it's impossible to completely eliminate the risk of phone scams, you can take proactive steps to minimize your vulnerability. Here are some effective prevention measures:

Remember, scammers are constantly evolving their tactics, so it's essential to remain vigilant and skeptical when it comes to unsolicited phone calls. By following the tips and strategies outlined in this chapter, you'll be better equipped to protect yourself from falling victim to phone scams and maintain your peace of mind. As the old saying goes, "Better safe than scammed!"

Chapter 6: Email Scams

Introduction:

In today's digital age, email has become an integral part of our personal and professional lives. Unfortunately, it has also become a prime target for scammers and cyber criminals. Email scams, such as phishing attacks and email spoofing, can be highly deceptive and can cause significant harm if not recognized and dealt with appropriately. In this chapter, we will explore various types of email scams, learn how to avoid falling victim to them, and discover practical steps to secure our email accounts.

Phishing Attacks and Email Spoofing

Phishing attacks are one of the most common types of email scams. These attacks involve tricking individuals into revealing sensitive information, such as passwords, credit card details, or social security numbers, by impersonating a trusted entity. The scammers often send emails that appear to be from reputable organizations, such as banks, online retailers, or government agencies. These emails typically contain urgent requests for personal information or require the recipient to click on a malicious link.

Anecdote:
I recently received an email that appeared to be from my bank, informing me that there was suspicious activity on my account. The email urged me to click on a link to verify my information and prevent any unauthorized access.

However, something seemed off about the email. The logo looked slightly distorted, and the email address had a few extra characters. Trusting my gut feeling, I decided to contact my bank directly to inquire about the email. As it turns out, it was indeed a phishing attempt, and I narrowly avoided falling into the scammer's trap.

Preventative   Measures:
- Be cautious of emails requesting personal information, especially if they claim to be urgent or   threatening.
- Double-check the email address of the sender. Phishing emails often use similar, but slightly altered, addresses to deceive recipients.
- Hover over links before clicking on them to verify their destination. If the URL looks suspicious or unrelated to the email's content, refrain   from   clicking.
- Install reputable anti-phishing software that can detect and block fraudulent emails.

Avoiding Suspicious Email Attachments

Email attachments can be a convenient way to share files, documents, or photos. However, scammers often exploit this feature to distribute malware, ransomware, or other malicious software. Opening an infected attachment can lead to the compromise of your computer's security and the loss of sensitive data.

Research   Finding:
According to a study conducted by cybersecurity firm Symantec, 94% of malware is delivered via email attachments. This statistic emphasizes the importance of being cautious when opening attachments, even if they appear to be from a trusted source.

Protective   Measures:
- Avoid opening email attachments from unknown senders or suspicious emails that you were   not   expecting.

- Scan all attachments with up-to-date antivirus software before opening them.
- If in doubt, contact the sender directly to confirm the legitimacy of the attachment.
- Consider using cloud storage services or file-sharing platforms instead of email attachments for sharing large files.

Recognizing Fake Email Requests

Scammers are becoming increasingly sophisticated in their attempts to deceive email recipients. They may send emails that appear to be from a friend, colleague, or family member, requesting money, personal information, or other favors. These emails are often crafted to create a sense of urgency or exploit emotions, making it more challenging to spot the scam.

Practical   Step:

To determine the authenticity of an email, think critically and ask yourself the following questions:

1. Does the email sound like something the supposed sender would say? Look for any unusual language or tone that may indicate a scam.

2. Is the request out of character for the sender? If the email asks for money or personal information unexpectedly, it is worth investigating further.

3. Can you verify the sender's identity through another communication channel? Reach out to the person directly through a phone call or a separate email to confirm the request.

Secondary Heading: Steps to Secure Your Email Account

Securing your email account is crucial to protect your personal information and prevent scammers from accessing your contacts or using your account to spread malicious content. Here are a few steps you can take to enhance the security of your email account:

Inspirational   Quote: "Vigilance is the key to a secure email account. Stay alert, question everything, and never underestimate the creativity of scammers." - Unknown

Remember, email scams are constantly evolving, and scammers are always looking for new ways to deceive unsuspecting individuals. By staying informed, practicing caution, and implementing security measures, you can protect yourself from falling victim to email scams.

Chapter 7: Social Engineering Scams

In this chapter, we will delve into the world of social engineering scams, where scammers manipulate individuals into revealing sensitive information or performing actions that they normally wouldn't. Social engineering is a psychological tactic used to exploit human vulnerabilities, and it is essential for consumers to be aware of these techniques in order to protect themselves from falling victim to these scams.

Understanding Manipulative Tactics

Social engineering scams rely on the art of manipulation, preying on our natural instincts and emotions. Scammers use various tactics to gain our trust and cooperation, such as impersonating trusted individuals or organizations, creating a sense of urgency or fear, or appealing to our desire for rewards or recognition. By understanding these tactics, we can better identify and resist their influence.

For example, let's say you receive a call from someone claiming to be from your bank, urgently requesting your account details. They might create a sense of fear by stating that your account has been compromised and that immediate action is required to prevent further damage. In this situation, it's important to take a step back and verify the legitimacy of the call before providing any information. Remember, a reputable bank would never ask for sensitive information over the phone.

Recognizing Social Engineering Techniques

Scammers employ a range of techniques to manipulate their targets. Some common social engineering techniques include:

Phishing Attacks and Email Spoofing

Phishing attacks involve sending fraudulent emails that appear to be from reputable sources, such as banks or online retailers. These emails typically contain links or attachments that, when clicked, lead to fake websites or malware installation. By closely examining the sender's email address, checking for grammatical errors, and being cautious of unsolicited emails, you can avoid falling victim to phishing scams.

Avoiding Suspicious Email Attachments

Scammers often send emails with malicious attachments disguised as important documents or invoices. These attachments can contain malware or ransomware that can compromise your computer or personal information. It is crucial to never open attachments from unknown sources and to always verify the legitimacy of the sender before taking any action.

Recognizing Fake Email Requests

Scammers may pose as trusted individuals or organizations, requesting sensitive information or immediate action. They often create a sense of urgency or fear to pressure their targets into complying. To protect yourself, always verify the authenticity of the request by contacting the sender directly through a trusted channel, such as their official website or phone number.

Steps to Secure Your Email Account

To safeguard your email account from social engineering scams, consider implementing the following security measures:

Preventing Identity Theft

Identity theft is a severe consequence of falling victim to social engineering scams. Scammers can use your personal information to commit fraud, open accounts in your name, or even steal your identity. To prevent identity theft, it is essential to:

Building Stronger Security Habits

Developing strong security habits is crucial in protecting yourself from social engineering scams. Some practical steps to consider include:

Remember, scammers are continuously evolving their tactics, so it's essential to remain vigilant and continually update your knowledge to stay one step ahead.

Chapter 8: Awareness in Digital Interactions

In this digital age, our interactions have become increasingly reliant on screens and devices. From social media to online shopping, our personal information is constantly being shared and accessed. It is crucial to develop a strong awareness of the potential risks and vulnerabilities that come with these interactions. In this chapter, we will explore practical steps to enhance our digital security and protect our personal information.

Verifying Online Identities

With the rise of social media and online communities, it has become easier for scammers to create fake identities and deceive unsuspecting individuals. To protect yourself, always verify the authenticity of the person or organization you are interacting with online. Look for verifying factors such as a verified badge on social media platforms or a professional website with contact information. If something feels off or too good to be true, trust your instincts and proceed with caution.

Education on Privacy Settings

Most online platforms provide privacy settings that allow you to control the visibility of your personal information. Take the time to familiarize yourself with these settings and adjust them according to your comfort level. Limit the amount of personal information you share publicly, such as your address or phone number. Regularly review and update your privacy settings to ensure they align with your desired level of privacy.

Taking Preemptive Security Measures

Protecting your personal information should be a top priority when engaging in digital interactions. Consider implementing the following preemptive security measures:

Navigating Social Media Safely

Social media platforms are a popular target for scammers due to the wealth of personal information available. To navigate social media safely, consider the following tips:

Remember, digital interactions can be both convenient and risky. By being aware of the potential risks and taking proactive steps to protect your personal information, you can navigate the digital landscape with confidence and peace of mind.

Chapter 9: Suspicious Signs and Red Flags

In this chapter, we will explore the various suspicious signs and red flags that can help you identify potential scams. By being aware of these warning signs, you can protect yourself from falling victim to manipulative tactics and fraudulent schemes.

Unusual Requests and Demands

One of the key red flags to watch out for is when someone makes unusual requests or demands. Scammers often try to exploit your trust and goodwill by asking for personal information, money, or access to your accounts. For example, if someone you just met online asks for your social security number or requests that you wire them money, it's important to be skeptical. Remember, legitimate individuals or organizations would rarely make such requests without a valid reason.

To avoid falling for these scams, it's crucial to be cautious and question the intentions behind these requests. Always take the time to verify the legitimacy of the person or organization before sharing any sensitive information or fulfilling any unusual demands.

Pressures to Act Quickly

Scammers often use high-pressure tactics to create a sense of urgency and force you into making impulsive decisions. They may claim that you have won a prize but need to act immediately to claim it, or they might threaten dire consequences if you don't comply with their demands. These tactics prey on our natural instinct to avoid missing out or facing negative outcomes.

To protect yourself, it's essential to recognize and resist these pressures to act quickly. Take a step back, gather more information, and consult with trusted individuals before making any major decisions. Remember, legitimate opportunities and offers will usually allow you time to consider and evaluate them thoroughly.

Spelling and Grammatical Errors

While it may seem trivial, paying attention to spelling and grammatical errors can provide valuable insights into the authenticity of a message or communication. Scammers often operate from countries where English may not be their first language, leading to noticeable mistakes in their writing.

If you receive an email, message, or any form of communication riddled with spelling and grammatical errors, it should raise your suspicions. Legitimate businesses and organizations typically take great care in presenting themselves professionally and would not make such glaring mistakes. Always be vigilant and skeptical when encountering these errors, as they can be a strong indication of a scam.

Phrases Used to Instill Fear or Urgency

Scammers are skilled at manipulating emotions and using fear or urgency to push their victims into taking action. They may use phrases like "your account has been compromised" or "immediate action required" to create a sense of panic and urgency. By instilling fear, scammers hope to bypass your rational thinking and prompt you to make impulsive decisions.

To avoid falling for these tactics, it's crucial to stay calm and level-headed. Take a moment to assess the situation objectively and critically evaluate the information presented to you. Remember, legitimate organizations would rarely communicate urgent matters through unsolicited emails or phone calls. When in doubt, always reach out to the official channels of the organization to verify the authenticity of the message.

By being aware of these suspicious signs and red flags, you can empower yourself to make informed decisions and protect yourself from scams. Remember, it's always better to err on the side of caution and trust your instincts. Stay vigilant, stay skeptical, and stay safe!

Chapter 10: Protecting Your Personal Information

In today's digital age, protecting your personal information is crucial to avoid falling victim to scams. With cybercriminals becoming increasingly sophisticated, it's important to take proactive steps to safeguard your sensitive data. In this chapter, we will explore practical strategies to protect your personal information and reduce the risk of being scammed.

Safe Handling of Personal Data

One of the first steps to protect your personal information is to be mindful of how you handle it. Whether it's online or offline, it's essential to adopt safe practices to prevent your data from falling into the wrong hands.

1. Be cautious with sharing information: Avoid sharing sensitive information, such as your Social Security number, bank account details, or home address, unless it is absolutely necessary. Scammers often exploit this information for identity theft or financial fraud.

2. Securely dispose of physical documents: Shred or destroy any documents that contain personal information before disposing of them. Dumpster diving is still a common tactic used by scammers to extract valuable data.

3. Use secure networks: When accessing the internet, be cautious about using public Wi-Fi networks, as they may not be secure. If you need to transmit sensitive information, consider using a virtual private network (VPN) to encrypt your data and protect your privacy.

4. Regularly update your devices: Keep your devices, including smartphones, tablets, and

computers, up to date with the latest security patches and software updates. These updates often contain important security fixes that can protect you from known vulnerabilities.

Securing Financial Information

Financial information is a prime target for scammers, as it can be used to carry out fraudulent activities. By implementing the following measures, you can minimize the risk of your financial information falling into the wrong hands.

1. Use secure websites: When making online purchases or accessing your bank accounts, ensure that the website is secure. Look for "https://" at the beginning of the URL and a padlock symbol in the address bar. These indicate

that the website has implemented SSL encryption, providing a secure connection.

2. Monitor your financial accounts: Regularly review your bank and credit card statements for any unusual or unauthorized transactions. If you spot any discrepancies, report them to your financial institution immediately.

3. Enable two-factor authentication: Two-factor authentication adds an extra layer of security to your online accounts by requiring an additional verification step, such as a unique code sent to your mobile device. Enable this feature whenever possible to protect your financial accounts.

4. Beware of phishing emails: Be cautious of emails requesting your financial information or login credentials. Legitimate organizations will never ask for sensitive information via email. If you receive such an email, contact the

organization directly using their official contact information to verify its authenticity.

Avoiding Oversharing Online

In today's interconnected world, it's easy to overshare personal information on social media platforms and other online platforms. However, this can make you an easy target for scammers. Here are some tips to avoid oversharing and protect your personal information online.

1. Review privacy settings: Regularly review and adjust the privacy settings on your social media accounts to restrict who can view your posts and personal information. Limit the visibility of your profile to only trusted friends and family.

2. Be mindful of what you post: Think twice before sharing personal details, such as your full

name, birthday, or current location, on social media. This information can be used by scammers to impersonate you or carry out identity theft.

3. Avoid accepting friend requests from strangers: Be cautious about accepting friend requests from individuals you don't know. Scammers often create fake profiles to gather information or trick you into revealing sensitive details.

4. Think before clicking on links: Be skeptical of links shared on social media or sent via email, especially if they appear suspicious or come from unknown sources. These links could lead to phishing websites or malware-infected downloads.

Utilizing Two-Factor Authentication

Two-factor authentication (2FA) is an effective security measure that adds an extra layer of protection to your online accounts. By requiring an additional verification step beyond just a password, 2FA significantly reduces the risk of unauthorized access. Here's how you can make the most of 2FA:

1. Enable 2FA on all your accounts: Whenever possible, enable 2FA on your online accounts, including email, social media, and financial platforms. Most major services offer this feature, and it's usually found in the account settings or security options.

2. Use app-based authentication: Instead of relying on SMS-based 2FA, which can be vulnerable to SIM card swapping, opt for app-based authentication methods like Google Authenticator or Authy. These apps generate

unique codes that are synchronized with your accounts, providing an additional layer of security.

3. Keep backup codes: When setting up 2FA, most services provide backup codes that can be used if you lose access to your authentication app or device. Store these codes securely, preferably in a password manager, to ensure you can regain access to your accounts if needed.

4. Stay vigilant against phishing attacks: Even with 2FA enabled, it's essential to remain cautious of phishing attacks. Scammers may attempt to trick you into revealing your authentication codes through deceptive emails or websites. Always verify the authenticity of requests before providing any sensitive information.

By implementing these personal information protection strategies, you can significantly reduce the risk of falling victim to scams. Remember, staying informed and adopting good security practices are essential in today's digital landscape. Stay vigilant, and don't let the scammers dupe you!

Chapter 11: Verification and Due Diligence

In a world where scams are becoming increasingly sophisticated, it is crucial for consumers to exercise caution and skepticism. One of the most effective ways to protect yourself from falling victim to scams is by conducting thorough verification and due diligence. In this chapter, we will explore the importance of checking credentials, researching businesses, questioning information, and consulting trusted sources.

Checking Credentials and Licenses

When dealing with professionals or businesses, it is essential to verify their credentials and licenses. Scammers often pose as experts in various fields, using fake credentials to deceive unsuspecting consumers. To avoid being duped, take the time to research and confirm the legitimacy of the person or company you are dealing with.

For example, imagine you are looking to hire a contractor to remodel your kitchen. You come across a website advertising a contractor who claims to have years of experience and numerous satisfied clients. Before proceeding, it would be wise to check if the contractor is licensed and registered with the appropriate authorities. This can be as simple as searching for their name in the database of licensed contractors in your area.

Researching Businesses and Websites

The internet has made it easier than ever for scammers to create fake businesses and websites that appear legitimate. To protect yourself, invest time in researching businesses and verifying their credibility. Look for online reviews, testimonials, and ratings from reputable sources. Check if the business has a physical address and contact information that can be verified.

Let's say you are considering purchasing a product from an online store you have never heard of before. Before completing the transaction, search for reviews of the store and see if other customers have had positive experiences. Look for any red flags, such as a lack of contact information or negative feedback indicating poor customer service.

Questioning Unverified Information

Scammers often rely on providing unverified information to manipulate their victims. To avoid being deceived, it is essential to question and verify any information that seems suspicious or too good to be true.

For instance, imagine you receive an email claiming that you have won a lottery prize, but you don't remember entering any lottery. Instead of immediately celebrating your newfound fortune, take a step back and critically evaluate the information. Ask yourself if this aligns with your previous actions and if it seems plausible. Remember, scammers prey on our emotions and desires, so maintaining a healthy skepticism is crucial.

Consulting Trusted Sources

When in doubt, seek advice and information from trusted sources. If something seems fishy or too good to be true, reach out to friends, family, or professionals who can provide guidance and a fresh perspective.

For example, imagine you receive a phone call from someone claiming to be from your bank, asking for sensitive personal information. Instead of hastily sharing your details, hang up and call your bank directly using the official contact information you have on record. Discuss the situation with a representative who can confirm if the call was legitimate or a scam attempt.

By consulting trusted sources, you can gain valuable insights and reassurance, helping you make informed decisions and avoid scams.

Verification and due diligence play a vital role in protecting yourself from scams. By checking credentials, researching businesses, questioning unverified information, and consulting trusted sources, you can significantly reduce your risk of falling victim to scams. Remember, scammers are constantly evolving, so it is essential to remain vigilant and skeptical. Trust your instincts, ask questions, and seek advice when needed. Together, we can combat scams and create a safer digital environment for all.

Chapter 12: Consultation and Second Opinions

When it comes to making important decisions, seeking advice from trusted individuals can be invaluable. This is especially true when it comes to avoiding scams. In Chapter 12, we will explore the importance of consultation and second opinions in protecting ourselves from scams.

Seeking Advice from Trusted Individuals

One of the first steps in avoiding scams is reaching out to people we trust. Whether it's a close friend, family member, or a financial advisor, their guidance can provide a fresh perspective and help us make informed choices. For example, let's consider a situation where you receive an email claiming that you won a lottery and need to send money to claim your prize. Consulting with a trusted individual can help you recognize the red flags and avoid falling into the scammer's trap.

Importance of Independent Verification

While seeking advice from trusted individuals is crucial, it's equally important to independently verify the information we receive. This can involve conducting research, fact-checking, and consulting reliable sources. For instance, if you receive a phone call from someone claiming to be a representative from a reputable company, take the time to verify their identity by reaching out to the company directly. This simple step can save you from becoming a victim of a phone scam.

Recognizing Biases and Manipulation

Scammers are masters of manipulation, and they often exploit our emotions and vulnerabilities to deceive us. By consulting with trusted individuals, we can gain insights into our own biases and blind spots. These trusted individuals can help us recognize when we may be too emotionally invested or susceptible to a scam. Let's say you receive an unsolicited email offering a once-in-a-lifetime investment opportunity. Consulting with a trusted financial advisor can help you see through the scammer's enticing promises and avoid making impulsive decisions.

Building a Support Network

Another benefit of seeking consultation and second opinions is that it allows us to build a support network. By surrounding ourselves with knowledgeable and trustworthy individuals, we create a safety net that can catch us when we're about to fall for a scam. This network not only provides us with guidance and advice but also serves as a source of encouragement and reassurance. Together, we can navigate the complex landscape of scams and protect ourselves.

In conclusion, consultation and second opinions play a crucial role in scam prevention. By seeking advice from trusted individuals, independently verifying information, recognizing biases, and building a support network, we can enhance our ability to make informed choices and avoid falling victim to scams. Remember, it's always better to consult and seek second opinions than to go it alone. As the saying goes, "Two heads are better than one."

Chapter 13: Interviews with Fraud Victims

In this chapter, we will delve into the personal experiences of individuals who have fallen victim to scams. By hearing their stories and learning from their mistakes, we can gain valuable insights into the tactics used by scammers and the emotional impact of being scammed. Through these interviews, we hope to provide support and guidance to those who have been affected, as well as empower readers to take preventative measures to avoid falling into similar traps.

Understanding Personal Experiences

Every scam victim has a unique story to tell, but there are common threads that run through their experiences. By listening to their narratives, we can gain a deeper understanding of the vulnerabilities that scammers exploit and the consequences of their actions. These interviews shed light on the emotional toll of being deceived and the challenges faced during the recovery process.

One interviewee, Jane, shared her experience of falling for an investment scam. She was promised high returns on her investment and was convinced by the scammer's persuasive tactics. Jane invested a significant sum of money, only to later discover that the investment opportunity was a complete fraud. She suffered not only financial losses but also emotional distress and a sense of betrayal.

Learning from Mistakes and Regrets

Interviews with fraud victims provide an opportunity to learn from their mistakes and regrets. By understanding the warning signs they missed or the decisions they wish they had made differently, readers can gain valuable insights into how to protect themselves from similar scams.

Another interviewee, John, shared his regret about not conducting proper due diligence before making an online purchase. He fell victim to a fake online store that offered attractive discounts on popular products. Despite feeling a nagging suspicion, John ignored the red flags and proceeded with the purchase. The product never arrived, and his money was gone. John now emphasizes the importance of researching online stores, reading reviews, and ensuring secure payment options before making any purchases.

Emotional Impact of Being Scammed

Scams not only have financial consequences but also take a toll on victims' emotional well-being. Understanding the emotional impact is crucial for both victims and those seeking to support them. By sharing these stories, we aim to provide comfort to victims and help them navigate the healing process.

One interviewee, Sarah, shared the profound sense of shame and embarrassment she felt after falling for a phone scam. The scammer convinced her to disclose personal information by posing as a trusted authority figure. Sarah blamed herself for being fooled and had difficulty trusting others afterward. Through therapy and support groups, she was able to regain her confidence and learn to forgive herself.

Recovery and Coping Strategies

Recovering from a scam can be a challenging journey, but it is possible to move forward and regain control. In this section, we will explore the strategies employed by victims to rebuild their lives and protect themselves from future scams.

During an interview, Mark shared his experience of being a victim of an email phishing scam. The scammer gained access to his email account and used it to deceive his contacts. Mark took immediate action by changing his password, enabling two-factor authentication, and warning his contacts about the scam. He also sought assistance from his email provider's support team to ensure the security of his account. Mark's proactive approach helped him regain control and prevented further damage.

Remember, you are not alone if you have been scammed. By sharing these stories and strategies, we hope to empower readers to take action, seek support, and recover from the emotional and financial impact of scams.

Chapter 14: Reporting and Complaining

Reporting and complaining about scams is an essential step in combating fraud and seeking justice. By taking action and alerting the relevant authorities, you not only protect yourself but also help prevent others from falling victim to the same scam. In this chapter, we will explore the steps you can take to report scams effectively and increase the chances of a successful investigation.

Identifying Relevant Authorities and Agencies

When you discover that you have been scammed, it's crucial to report the incident to the appropriate authorities and agencies. The specific organizations you should contact may vary depending on the type of scam and your location. Here are some common entities to consider:

- Local law enforcement: Start by contacting your local police department or sheriff's office. They can guide you through the process of filing a police report, which is an essential step in documenting the scam and initiating an investigation.

- Consumer protection agencies: Research the consumer protection agencies in your country or region. These organizations are dedicated to safeguarding consumers' rights and can assist in investigating and prosecuting scammers. Examples include the Federal Trade Commission (FTC) in the United States or the Competition and Consumer Protection Commission (CCPC) in Ireland.

- Better Business Bureau (BBB): If the scam involves a business, filing a complaint with the BBB can help raise awareness and potentially lead to the resolution of your issue. The BBB acts as a mediator between consumers and businesses and can help facilitate communication and resolution.

- Financial institutions: If the scam involves financial transactions, contact your bank or credit card company immediately. They can guide you through the process of disputing charges and potentially recovering funds.

- Internet Crime Complaint Center (IC3): For online scams, consider reporting the incident to the IC3. It's a partnership between the Federal Bureau of Investigation (FBI) and the National White Collar Crime Center (NW3C), dedicated to receiving and analyzing internet crime complaints.

Providing Accurate and Detailed Information

When reporting a scam, it's crucial to provide accurate and detailed information to the authorities or agencies you contact. Here are some essential details to include:

Documenting Evidence for Investigations

To maximize the chances of a successful investigation, it's essential to document and preserve any evidence related to the scam. Here are some steps you can take:

Seeking Legal Assistance if Necessary

In some cases, it may be necessary to seek legal assistance to recover your losses or take legal action against the scammer. Here are a few situations where consulting with a lawyer may be beneficial:

- Complex scams: If the scam involved intricate legal or financial arrangements, seeking legal advice can help you navigate the complexities and protect your rights.

- International scams: If the scam originated from another country, consult with a lawyer experienced in international law. They can guide you through the process of pursuing legal action across borders.

- Class-action lawsuits: If multiple individuals were affected by the same scam, joining or initiating a class-action lawsuit can increase the chances of recovering your losses and holding the scammer accountable.

Remember, seeking legal assistance doesn't necessarily mean you have to take legal action. A lawyer can provide valuable advice and help you explore the available options based on your specific circumstances.

Reporting and complaining about scams is a powerful way to fight back against fraudsters and protect yourself and others from falling victim to their schemes. By identifying the relevant authorities, providing accurate information, documenting evidence, and seeking legal assistance when needed, you can play an active role in combating scams and promoting a safer consumer environment. Remember, your actions may not only bring justice but also contribute to the prevention of future scams.

Chapter 15: Emerging Scam Trends

In this chapter, we will explore the ever-evolving landscape of scams and the importance of staying informed about new fraud methods. As technology advances, scammers find new ways to exploit vulnerabilities and deceive unsuspecting consumers. By understanding emerging scam trends, we can adapt our prevention strategies and protect ourselves and our loved ones.

Staying Updated on New Fraud Methods

Scammers are constantly refining their tactics and finding innovative ways to deceive consumers. It is crucial to stay informed about the latest scam trends to recognize and avoid potential threats. One emerging scam trend is the rise of deep fake technology, which allows scammers to create realistic videos or audios impersonating someone else. These deep fake scams can be used for various purposes, such as blackmail or spreading false information. By staying updated on new fraud methods, we can be more vigilant and discerning when encountering suspicious content.

To keep yourself informed, consider subscribing to reputable cybersecurity blogs or newsletters. These sources often provide timely updates on emerging scam trends and offer practical tips for prevention. Additionally, follow trusted organizations and experts on social media platforms, as they often share valuable insights and warnings about new scams. By staying connected to the cybersecurity community, you can stay one step ahead of scammers.

Analysis of Recent Scam Cases

Examining recent scam cases can provide valuable insights into the techniques used by scammers and the vulnerabilities they exploit. Let's take a closer look at a recent scam involving fraudulent tech support calls.

Case Study: The Tech Support Scam

In this scam, victims receive unsolicited phone calls from individuals claiming to be tech support representatives from well-known companies, such as Microsoft or Apple. The scammers use various tactics to convince the victims that their computers are infected with viruses or experiencing technical issues. They often ask for remote access to the victim's computer or request payment for their services.

To prevent falling victim to this scam, it is essential to remember that legitimate tech support representatives will never initiate contact with you unsolicited. Always be skeptical of unexpected calls claiming to be from tech support. If you have concerns about your computer's security or performance, contact the company directly using their official contact information.

Adapting Prevention Strategies

As scams evolve, so should our prevention strategies. Here are some practical steps you can take to adapt your approach:

Collaborating to Combat Scams

Combating scams requires a collective effort from individuals, organizations, and policymakers. By working together, we can create a safer digital environment for everyone. Here are some ways we can collaborate:

By collaborating and sharing resources, we can work towards a future where scams are less prevalent and consumers are better protected.

Remember, staying updated on emerging scam trends is essential in our ongoing battle against fraud. By adapting our prevention strategies and collaborating with others, we can create a safer digital world for ourselves and future generations.

Chapter 16: Digital Security Measures

In today's digital landscape, protecting our personal information and online presence is of utmost importance. With the ever-evolving tactics of scammers and cybercriminals, it's crucial to implement robust digital security measures to safeguard ourselves from potential scams. In this chapter, we will explore some practical steps and tools that can help enhance our online security and protect against various digital threats.

Using Antivirus and Anti-malware Software

One of the fundamental steps in digital security is investing in reliable antivirus and anti-malware software. These tools act as a shield, continuously scanning your computer or device for any malicious software or viruses. By regularly updating your antivirus software and running scheduled scans, you can detect and eliminate potential threats before they cause any harm.

Anecdote: I once received an email with an enticing subject line claiming that I had won a free vacation. Curiosity got the best of me, and I clicked on a link in the email which led to a website full of malware. Thankfully, my antivirus software immediately flagged it and prevented any harm to my computer.

Secure Browsing and Network Protection

When browsing the internet, it's essential to practice safe browsing habits and utilize network protection measures. Here are a few tips:

1. Use HTTPS: Always ensure that the websites you visit use HTTPS encryption. This encryption protocol safeguards your information while transmitting it over the internet, making it harder for hackers to intercept and steal your data.

2. Avoid Public Wi-Fi: Public Wi-Fi networks are often unsecured, making them a playground for hackers. Try to avoid accessing sensitive information or making online transactions when connected to public Wi-Fi. If you must use it, consider utilizing a virtual private network (VPN) to encrypt your data and protect your online activities.

3. Keep Your Firewall Enabled: Firewalls act as a barrier between your computer and the internet, monitoring incoming and outgoing network traffic. Keeping your firewall enabled provides an additional layer of protection against unauthorized access and potential attacks.

Creating Strong and Unique Passwords

Passwords are the keys to our online accounts, and creating strong and unique passwords is essential to prevent unauthorized access. Here are some tips for creating secure passwords:

1. Length and Complexity: Aim for passwords that are at least 12 characters long and include a combination of uppercase and lowercase letters, numbers, and special characters. Avoid using easily guessable information like birthdates or pet names.

2. Unique for Each Account: It's crucial to use a different password for each online account. If one account gets compromised, using the same password for other accounts puts them at risk as well. Consider utilizing a password manager to securely store and generate unique passwords for each account.

3. Two-Factor Authentication (2FA): Enable two-factor authentication whenever possible. This adds an extra layer of security by requiring a second form of verification, such as a unique code sent to your mobile device, in addition to your password.

Research Finding: According to a study conducted by the National Cyber Security Centre, using a combination of three random words as a password is both memorable and secure. For example, "correcthorsebatterystaple" is much stronger than a shorter password with complex characters.

Encrypting Sensitive Data

Encrypting sensitive data ensures that even if it falls into the wrong hands, it remains unreadable and inaccessible. Here are a few methods to consider:

1. Full Disk Encryption: Encrypt your entire hard drive to protect all the data stored on your computer. Most modern operating systems offer built-in disk encryption features, such as BitLocker for Windows and FileVault for Mac.

2. Secure Messaging Apps: When sharing sensitive information online or via messaging apps, opt for platforms that offer end-to-end encryption. This means that only the intended recipient can decrypt and read the messages.

3. Password-Protect Documents: Before sharing or storing sensitive documents, consider password-protecting them. This adds an extra

layer of security, even if someone gains access to the file.

Implementing these digital security measures can significantly reduce the risk of falling victim to online scams and cyber attacks. By staying vigilant and regularly updating your security software, you are taking proactive steps to protect your digital identity and personal information.

Chapter 17: Educating Others

In this chapter, we will explore the importance of educating others about scams and how to promote awareness in our communities. By sharing our knowledge and experiences, we can empower others to make informed choices and protect themselves from falling victim to scams.

Teaching Friends and Family about Scams

One of the most effective ways to prevent scams is to educate our friends and family members about the common tactics used by scammers. We can start by sharing our own experiences or stories of others who have been scammed. By using real-life examples, we can help them understand the risks and consequences involved.

It's important to approach this conversation with empathy and understanding. Remember, not everyone may be aware of the various types of scams or the techniques used by scammers. Be patient and provide clear explanations, highlighting the red flags to watch out for.

To make the learning process more engaging, you can also incorporate interactive activities or quizzes. For example, you can create a game where you present different scenarios and ask them to identify whether it's a scam or not. This will not only make the learning experience fun but also help them develop critical thinking skills.

Promoting Awareness in the Community

In addition to educating our friends and family, we can also play an active role in promoting scam awareness within our communities. By organizing workshops or seminars, we can reach a larger audience and create a safe space for discussions.

When planning these events, consider inviting experts in the field of cybersecurity or local law enforcement agencies to share their insights. Their expertise and real-life examples will add credibility to the information shared and help participants understand the gravity of the issue.

To make these events more engaging, you can also invite scam victims who have successfully recovered from their experiences. Their personal stories of resilience and overcoming adversity can inspire others and provide hope in challenging times.

Participating in Prevention Campaigns

Another way to educate others is to actively participate in scam prevention campaigns. Many organizations and government agencies run campaigns to raise awareness about scams and provide resources for prevention. By getting involved, we can contribute to the collective effort of combating scams.

You can start by sharing information about these campaigns on your social media platforms or personal blog. Use catchy slogans or hashtags to grab attention and encourage others to join the cause. Remember, the more people we reach, the greater the impact we can make.

Additionally, you can volunteer your time to speak at schools or community centers. By delivering engaging presentations and interactive workshops, you can equip young individuals with the knowledge and skills needed to protect themselves from scams. Remember, educating the younger generation is crucial as they are often targeted by scammers due to their lack of experience and vulnerability.

Empowering Others to Make Informed Choices

Ultimately, our goal in educating others about scams is to empower them to make informed choices. By providing them with the necessary knowledge and tools, we can help them navigate the digital landscape safely and confidently.

Encourage your friends and family to stay updated on the latest scam trends and prevention methods. Share reliable resources, such as reputable websites or government agencies that provide information on scams. Remind them to verify information before taking any action or sharing personal details online.

By empowering others, we create a network of vigilant individuals who can support each other in identifying and preventing scams. Together, we can build a stronger and more resilient community that is well-equipped to tackle the challenges posed by scammers.

Remember, education is key in the fight against scams. By sharing our knowledge and experiences, we can make a significant difference in the lives of others. Let's work together to create a scam-free future for everyone.

Chapter 18: Building Resilience and Trust

In this chapter, we will explore the importance of building resilience and trust after falling victim to a scam. It is natural to feel a range of emotions such as anger, embarrassment, and betrayal, but it is essential to process these emotions and move forward with a renewed sense of confidence in online interactions.

Processing Emotional Responses to Scams

Being scammed can be a traumatic experience, leaving victims feeling vulnerable and violated. It is crucial to acknowledge and process these emotions rather than suppressing them. Talking to a trusted friend, family member, or therapist can provide a safe space to express your feelings and gain support.

Remember, you are not alone in this experience. Many individuals have fallen victim to scams, and sharing your story can help create a sense of community and healing.

Rebuilding Confidence in Online Interactions

After being scammed, it is natural to feel a sense of distrust towards online interactions. However, it is important to remember that not everyone online is malicious. By taking proactive steps to protect yourself, you can rebuild confidence and engage in safe online interactions.

Start by educating yourself about common scam tactics and red flags. This knowledge will empower you to recognize potential scams and avoid falling victim again. Additionally, practice good digital hygiene by regularly updating your software, using strong and unique passwords, and being cautious when sharing personal information.

Building Trustworthy Online Relationships

While it is essential to be cautious, it is equally important to foster trustworthy online relationships. Surround yourself with individuals who prioritize your safety and well-being. Engage in online communities that promote education and awareness about scams, and collaborate with others to combat fraudulent activities.

When engaging in online dating or social media interactions, take the time to get to know the person before fully trusting them. Look for consistency in their behavior and information shared. Trust should be built gradually and based on mutual respect and understanding.

Balancing Caution and Trust

Building resilience and trust after falling victim to a scam is all about finding the right balance between caution and trust. It is natural to be more cautious moving forward, but it is important not to let fear consume you. By taking proactive steps to protect yourself and staying informed about emerging scam trends, you can navigate online interactions with confidence.

Remember that trust is earned over time and through consistent actions. Be patient and allow trust to develop naturally, while always maintaining a healthy level of skepticism.

Practical Steps to Build Resilience and Trust:

Remember, building resilience and trust takes time and effort. By incorporating these practical steps into your life, you can regain confidence and protect yourself from future scams.

Chapter 19: Continual Vigilance

In this chapter, we will discuss the importance of maintaining continual vigilance in order to protect oneself from scams. We will explore the mindset and habits that can help individuals stay alert and skeptical, as well as the role of personal vulnerabilities in falling for scams. By reflecting on these factors and staying up-to-date on prevention methods, readers can develop a resilient and informed approach to online interactions.

Maintaining Alertness and Skepticism

Scammers are constantly evolving their tactics to deceive unsuspecting individuals. To stay one step ahead, it is crucial to maintain a mindset of alertness and skepticism. This means questioning information presented to you, double-checking facts, and being cautious of unexpected or too-good-to-be-true offers.

Anecdote: John, a tech-savvy individual, received an email from what appeared to be his bank, alerting him of a security breach and requesting his account details. Instead of immediately responding, John took a moment to evaluate the situation. He noticed that the email had several grammatical errors and a suspicious email address. Upon further investigation, he discovered that it was a phishing attempt. By staying alert and skeptical, John prevented himself from falling victim to a scam.

Practical   Steps:
1. Always verify the authenticity of emails, messages, or phone calls before providing personal   information.
2. Be cautious of unsolicited offers or requests for money.
3. Examine websites and URLs for signs of phishing or fraudulent activity.

Recognizing Manipulative Techniques

Scammers are skilled at manipulating their targets, using psychological tactics to evoke fear, urgency, or trust. By understanding these techniques, individuals can better protect themselves from falling into the trap.

Anecdote: Sarah, a retiree, received a phone call from someone claiming to be a representative from the government, informing her that she owed a significant amount in taxes. The caller used aggressive language and threatened legal action if she didn't comply immediately. Feeling panicked, Sarah almost provided her financial information. However, she remembered reading about similar scams and realized that the tactics being used were manipulative. She hung up and reported the incident to the authorities.

Practical   Steps:
1. Be aware of high-pressure tactics designed to make you act quickly without thinking.
2. Take a step back and evaluate the situation before making any decisions.
3. Seek advice from trusted individuals or authorities if you feel unsure or threatened.

Keeping Up with Prevention Methods

Scammers are constantly adapting their approaches, utilizing new technologies and exploiting vulnerabilities. To effectively protect oneself, it is crucial to stay informed about the latest scam trends and prevention methods.

Anecdote: Lisa, an avid online shopper, received an email promotion for a heavily discounted product from a website she had never heard of before. Intrigued by the deal, she clicked on the link and made a purchase. Unfortunately, the website turned out to be a scam, and Lisa never received the product. Disappointed and frustrated, Lisa realized she should have been more cautious and researched the website beforehand.

Practical   Steps:
1. Regularly educate yourself about the latest scam techniques and stay updated on fraud news.
2. Take advantage of resources such as scam alert

websites and consumer protection agencies. 3. Share your knowledge with friends and family to help create a network of informed individuals.

Reflecting on Personal Vulnerabilities

Understanding your own vulnerabilities is a crucial aspect of scam prevention. Scammers often prey on emotions, such as fear, greed, or loneliness. By recognizing and addressing these vulnerabilities, individuals can build resilience against manipulative tactics.

Anecdote: Mark, a recent divorcee, joined an online dating platform in search of companionship. He quickly formed a connection with someone who claimed to be a wealthy, successful individual. Despite warnings from friends, Mark became emotionally invested and eventually sent money to his newfound love interest. It was only later that he discovered he had fallen victim to a romance scam. Reflecting on his experience, Mark realized his vulnerability stemmed from a deep desire for companionship.

Practical   Steps:
1. Be aware of your emotional state and how it may impact your decision-making.
2. Seek support from trusted friends or professionals if you are feeling vulnerable or lonely.
3. Take the time to evaluate potential risks and consider the consequences before making any financial or personal decisions.

By maintaining alertness, recognizing manipulative techniques, staying informed, and reflecting on personal vulnerabilities, readers can develop a strong defense against scams. Continual vigilance is key to protecting oneself and others from falling victim to fraud. Remember, scams may be ever-present, but with the right mindset and knowledge, you can navigate the digital world safely. Stay vigilant and stay safe!

Chapter 20: Conclusion and Call to Action

Congratulations! You have made it to the end of this book, and now you are armed with valuable knowledge and strategies to protect yourself from scams. But before we part ways, let's recap the key learnings and discuss the importance of taking action to combat scams.

Summary of Key Learnings

Throughout this book, we have explored various types of scams, such as online dating scams, online shopping scams, phone scams, email scams, and social engineering scams. We have learned how scammers use psychological manipulation and exploit our vulnerabilities to deceive us. By recognizing the warning signs and adopting protective measures, we can significantly reduce the risk of falling for scams.

We have discussed the importance of consumer awareness and the consequences of falling for scams. We have explored practical steps to protect our personal information, verify the legitimacy of businesses and websites, and seek independent verification. We have also learned how to report scams and stay updated on emerging scam trends. In addition, we have delved into digital security measures and the importance of educating others to create a safer online environment.

Importance of Consumer Advocacy

Now that you have the knowledge and tools to protect yourself from scams, it's crucial to become an advocate for consumer protection. By sharing what you have learned with friends, family, and your community, you can help others avoid falling victim to scams. Education is key in preventing scams, and by participating in prevention campaigns and promoting awareness, you can make a significant impact.

Making Scam Prevention a Priority

Scam prevention should be a priority in our lives. It's not enough to simply be aware of scams; we must actively implement preventive measures and stay vigilant. By continually educating ourselves and keeping up with the latest scam trends, we can adapt our strategies and protect ourselves from evolving fraud methods. Remember, prevention is always better than cure.

Encouraging Policy Changes and Regulation

As individuals, we can make a difference in the fight against scams, but it's also crucial to advocate for policy changes and regulation. The more we raise awareness about scams and their detrimental effects, the more likely policymakers and authorities will take action. By reporting scams and providing accurate and detailed information, we contribute to investigations and help bring scammers to justice.

Take Action Today!

In conclusion, I urge you to take action against scams. Use the knowledge and strategies you have gained from this book to protect yourself and your loved ones. Share your experiences, educate others, and advocate for consumer protection. Together, we can build a safer online environment and empower individuals to make informed choices.

Remember, scams thrive in secrecy and ignorance. By shining a light on their tactics and sharing our knowledge, we weaken their power and protect ourselves and others from falling victim. Stay alert, stay informed, and stay safe.